PRAYERSCRIPTS
SPEAKING GOD'S WORD BACK TO HIM

SCRIPTURES & PRAYERS FOR
DELIVERANCE
FROM TROUBLE

40 DAYS OF PRAYER FOR
WHEN LIFE FEELS OVERWHELMING

CYRIL OPOKU

Scriptures & Prayers for Deliverance from Trouble: 40 Days of Prayer for When Life Feels Overwhelming

© 2025 Cyril Opoku. *PrayerScripts*. All rights reserved.

No part of this publication may be reproduced, stored in a retrieval system, or transmitted in any form or by any means—electronic, mechanical, photocopy, recording, or otherwise—without the prior written permission of the publisher, except in the case of brief quotations used in reviews, articles, or devotionals.

Published by *Quest Publications*

ISBN: 978-1-988439-56-3

Cover design by *Quest Publications (questpublications@outlook.com)*

Unless otherwise indicated, all Scripture quotations are taken from the World English Bible (WEB), which is in the public domain. For more information, visit: www.worldenglish.bible

This book is a work of devotional encouragement. It is not intended to replace biblical study, pastoral counsel, or professional therapy.

Printed in the United States of America.

First Edition: July 2016

Second Edition: June 2025

For more books like this, visit *PrayerScripts:* https://prayerscripts.org

Contents

Preface v
How to Use This Devotional vi

Day 1: Revive Me, Lord 1
Day 2: When My Heart Feels Heavy 2
Day 3: Because I Love You 3
Day 4: Chains Are Breaking 4
Day 5: You Lift My Head 5
Day 6: Surrounded but Safe 7
Day 7: Out of Trouble, Into Peace 8
Day 8: Victory Through You 9
Day 9: Hidden in Your Grace 10
Day 10: The Hands That Heal 11
Day 11: Call and I Will Answer 12
Day 12: Too Weak to Fight, Strong Enough to Pray 13
Day 13: When the Night Won't End 14
Day 14: May God Meet You There 15
Day 15: Safe in His Name 16
Day 16: Unshaken in the Storm 17
Day 17: Lifted High, Held Close 18
Day 18: Strength in the Struggle 19
Day 19: Blessed to Bless 20
Day 20: Freedom is Coming 21

Day 21:	Hope in the Silence	23
Day 22:	Lift Me from the Gates	24
Day 23:	Mercy in My Mess	25
Day 24:	Refuge in the Tears	27
Day 25:	Trust Through the Trial	29
Day 26:	Rise Up, God	31
Day 27:	Not a Stranger to My Sorrow	32
Day 28:	Beauty for Ashes	33
Day 29:	Double for My Trouble	34
Day 30:	Restored by Grace	35
Day 31:	Refined and Redeemed	36
Day 32:	Hope Beyond the Dust	37
Day 33:	Peace in the Quiet	39
Day 34:	Songs from the Wilderness	40
Day 35:	Valley of Rest	41
Day 36:	Faithful Way Out	42
Day 37:	Power in the Pressure	43
Day 38:	Comfort for the Weary	44
Day 39:	Crushed but Carried	45
Day 40:	When Trouble Finds Me	47
Epilogue		48

Preface

There are seasons in life when the weight of trouble feels too much to carry—when hope feels far, faith feels thin, and it's hard to even find the words to pray. If you've ever found yourself there, you're not alone. This book was born out of that sacred place—where human weakness meets divine strength.

Scriptures & Prayers for Deliverance from Trouble is not a manual for perfect faith, but a companion for real, raw, and honest moments. Over the course of 40 days, this devotional invites you into a daily rhythm of Scripture-based prayers, anchored in the truth of God's Word and spoken from the heart of someone who knows what it's like to cry out for help.

Each day includes a focused theme, a heartfelt prayer written in the first person, and a guiding Scripture—so you can pour out your heart to God and be reminded that He hears you, sees you, and delivers you. Whether you're walking through hardship, wrestling with anxiety, or simply weary from the battles of life, these prayers are meant to be your lifeline—honest words when your own words feel hard to find.

This book is one of the *PrayerScripts* devotional series—a collection designed to help you speak truth to your soul, connect with God personally, and find peace even in the middle of the storm.

I pray these pages become a space of healing, comfort, and renewed strength. May each day draw you closer to the One who is not only able to deliver—but willing, present, and faithful.

Because trouble doesn't get the final say. God does.

In His hope, Cyril O. (June 2025)

How to Use This Devotional

This 40-day devotional is designed to be both personal and flexible—something you can lean on in quiet moments, desperate prayers, or daily time with God. Here's how you can make the most of it:

1. **Set Aside Sacred Time**
   Choose a time each day—morning, evening, or during a lunch break—when you can pause, reflect, and invite God into your space. Even ten focused minutes can create room for His peace.

2. **Start with the Scripture**
   Each day begins with a key Scripture that anchors the theme. Read it slowly. Read it aloud. Let it speak to your soul before you move on. You may want to journal or underline words that stand out.

3. **Pray the Prayer Personally**
   The prayer that follows is written in the first person—so you can pray it as your own. Speak it aloud or silently from your heart. Let the words give voice to what you may struggle to say on your own.

4. **Linger with God**
   After the prayer, pause. Breathe. Listen. Let the Spirit bring peace, conviction, healing, or comfort. Some days may feel emotional—others may feel calm. Trust that God meets you either way.

5. **Return When Needed**
   These prayers aren't just for a one-time journey. Revisit them when life gets heavy again. Mark the ones that resonate most. Share them with someone who needs strength.

This devotional is not about perfect discipline—it's about consistent grace. Whether you journey through all 40 days in a row or return whenever trouble rises, may these Scriptures and prayers be a light in your darkness, a comfort in your distress, and a steady reminder that **God is with you, for you, and working through it all.**

You're not alone. Let's walk this journey together—one prayer at a time.

Day 1: Revive Me, Lord

> Revive me, Yahweh, for your name's sake. In your righteousness, bring my soul out of trouble.
> —Psalms 143:11 WEB

Heavenly Father,

Quicken me, O Lord, for Your name's sake. Breathe Your life into my weary soul. You see the places in me that feel empty, the burdens I carry that threaten to crush my spirit. I come to You not because I've earned it, but because of who You are—righteous, faithful, and full of mercy.

For the sake of Your righteousness, bring my soul out of trouble. Where I am anxious, bring peace. Where I am overwhelmed, bring stillness. Where I am lost, lead me back to You. Not for my glory, but for Yours—so that my life would be a testimony of Your grace and power.

I trust You, Lord. Do what only You can do—revive me, rescue me, and restore me.

In Jesus' name,
Amen.

Day 2: When My Heart Feels Heavy

> The troubles of my heart are enlarged. Oh bring me out of my distresses. Consider my affliction and my travail. Forgive all my sins. Consider my enemies, for they are many. They hate me with cruel hatred. Oh keep my soul, and deliver me. Let me not be disappointed, for I take refuge in you.
> —Psalms 25:17-20 WEB

Lord God,

The troubles of my heart are enlarged—I'm overwhelmed, and I don't always know what to do. I bring my fears, my confusion, and my pain before You now. Please, Lord, bring me out of my distresses. Reach into the deep places of my heart where no one else can go, and speak peace.

Look upon my affliction and my pain. You see what I carry—the wounds, the regrets, the struggles that weigh me down. Forgive all my sins, Lord. I know I fall short, but I also know Your mercy is greater.

I feel surrounded at times by things I can't control—by fears, by pressures, by people who don't understand. Guard my soul and deliver me. I take refuge in You, Lord. I trust You. Don't let me be ashamed for hoping in You. Hold me steady when everything else feels shaky.

In Jesus' name, I pray,
Amen.

Day 3: Because I Love You

> "Because he has set his love on me, therefore I will deliver him. I will set him on high, because he has known my name. He will call on me, and I will answer him. I will be with him in trouble. I will deliver him, and honor him. I will satisfy him with long life, and show him my salvation."
> —Psalms 91:14-16 WEB

Most High God,

Because I have set my love upon You, I rest in the promise that You will deliver me. You know my name, You know my heart—and You are faithful. When the world shakes, You are my solid place. When fear whispers, You remind me I am Yours.

You said You will set me on high, because I have known Your name. So I call on You now—confident that You will answer. Be near to me in trouble. Walk with me through every storm, and let Your presence calm every fear.

Thank You for Your promise to deliver me and to honor me—not because I deserve it, but because You are good. Satisfy me with long life, Lord—not just in years, but in the richness of knowing You. Show me Your salvation in deeper ways every day.

I love You, Lord. I trust You. And I thank You for holding me close.

In Jesus' name,
Amen.

Day 4: Chains Are Breaking

> Then they cried to Yahweh in their trouble, and he saved them out of their distresses. He brought them out of darkness and the shadow of death, and broke away their chains. Let them praise Yahweh for his loving kindness, for his wonderful deeds to the children of men! For he has broken the gates of brass, and cut through bars of iron.
> —Psalms 107:13-16 WEB

Gracious Father,

When I cried out to You in my trouble, You heard me. You didn't turn away or leave me in the dark—you brought me out of my distress. Thank You for Your mercy that meets me right where I am.

You broke through the chains I couldn't break on my own. You brought me out of the shadow, out of the prison of fear, sin, and sorrow. You shattered the gates of bronze and cut through the bars of iron. Nothing is too strong for You—not even the walls I built around my heart.

Lord, I praise You for being my Deliverer. You are the One who rescues and restores. Help me to walk in the freedom You've given me, and never forget the power of Your love.

In Jesus' name,
Amen.

Day 5: You Lift My Head

A Psalm by David, when he fled from Absalom his son. Yahweh, how my adversaries have increased! Many are those who rise up against me. Many there are who say of my soul, "There is no help for him in God." Selah. But you, Yahweh, are a shield around me, my glory, and the one who lifts up my head. I cry to Yahweh with my voice, and he answers me out of his holy hill. Selah. I laid myself down and slept. I awakened; for Yahweh sustains me. I will not be afraid of tens of thousands of people who have set themselves against me on every side. Arise, Yahweh! Save me, my God! For you have struck all of my enemies on the cheek bone. You have broken the teeth of the wicked. Salvation belongs to Yahweh. Your blessing be on your people. Selah.
—Psalms 3:1-8 WEB

O Lord,

So many rise against me—so many voices, both outside and within, that say I have no hope. But I lift my eyes to You, my Shield, my Glory, the One who lifts my head when I'm bowed low in fear and shame.

When I cry to You, You hear me. Even in the middle of the storm, You answer from Your holy hill. I lay down and sleep, and I wake again—because You sustain me. You hold me together when everything feels like it's falling apart.

I will not be afraid of the enemies that surround me, of the battles I didn't ask for. Arise, O Lord! Save me, my God! You are my Defender, my Strength, and my Salvation.

I trust You, even when it's hard. Lift me up, fight for me, and let me rest in Your peace.

In Jesus' name,
Amen.

Day 6: Surrounded but Safe

> Though I walk in the middle of trouble, you will revive me. You will stretch out your hand against the wrath of my enemies. Your right hand will save me. Yahweh will fulfill that which concerns me; your loving kindness, Yahweh, endures forever. Don't forsake the works of your own hands.
> —Psalms 138:7-8 WEB

Lord,

Though I walk in the midst of trouble, I know You are with me. You will revive me—you will breathe life into places that feel worn out and tired. You stretch out Your hand against the anger of my enemies, and Your mighty right hand saves me.

Thank You for being my protector, my strength, and my peace. I don't have to fear what's around me, because You are within me. You are working in ways I can't always see, and I trust Your plan for my life.

Fulfill Your purpose in me, Lord. Don't let my pain be wasted. You said You would perfect all that concerns me. I hold on to that promise. Your mercy endures forever—please don't let go of me. I am Yours.

In Jesus' name,
Amen.

Day 7: Out of Trouble, Into Peace

> A righteous person is delivered out of trouble, and the wicked takes his place.
> —Proverbs 11:8 WEB

Righteous God,

Thank You for being my Deliverer—the One who sees the snares I cannot see and rescues me from harm. Your Word says the righteous is delivered out of trouble, and I cling to that promise today. Even when chaos surrounds me, You are my hiding place and my strength.

I trust that You are working behind the scenes, removing danger, guiding my steps, and turning things around for my good. Let me walk in integrity and trust, knowing that You protect those who belong to You.

Deliver me, Lord, not just from outward trouble, but from fear, doubt, and anything that pulls my heart away from You. Let Your justice prevail, and let Your peace guard my mind.

In Jesus' name,
Amen.

Day 8: Victory Through You

> Give us help against the enemy, for the help of man is vain. Through God, we will do valiantly. For it is he who will tread down our enemies.
> —Psalms 108:12-13 WEB

Mighty God,

Give us help from trouble, for the help of man is useless. We've tried to rely on our own strength, and it always falls short. But with You—there is power, victory, and hope. You are our true help, our Defender when everything else fails.

Through You, we will do valiantly. It's not by our ability, but by Your Spirit that we overcome. You go before us. You fight for us. You tread down every enemy that stands in the way of Your purpose.

So today, we put our trust in You alone. Strengthen our hearts, steady our steps, and let Your victory be seen in our lives.

In Jesus' name,
Amen.

Day 9: Hidden in Your Grace

> For this, let everyone who is godly pray to you in a time when you may be found. Surely when the great waters overflow, they shall not reach to him. You are my hiding place. You will preserve me from trouble. You will surround me with songs of deliverance. Selah.
> —Psalms 32:6-7 WEB

Faithful Father,

Let everyone who is godly come to You while You may be found. In my weakness, I run to You. In the flood of great waters—in the rush of chaos, fear, or regret—they will not come near me, because I am hidden in You.

You are my hiding place. You surround me with songs of deliverance even when I feel surrounded by pressure. You protect me, not just from danger, but from despair. You are my safe place, my peace, my rescue.

Thank You for being near, for covering me in mercy, and for never letting go. Teach me to stay close to You, to trust You in every season, and to rest in the safety of Your presence.

In Jesus' name,
Amen.

Day 10: The Hands That Heal

> For he wounds, and binds up. He injures, and his hands make whole. He will deliver you in six troubles; yes, in seven no evil shall touch you. In famine he will redeem you from death; in war, from the power of the sword. You shall be hidden from the scourge of the tongue, neither shall you be afraid of destruction when it comes.
> —Job 5:18-21 WEB

Lord God,

Even in the wounds, I know You are at work. For though You wound, You also heal. Though You may allow pain, Your hands are the ones that restore. I trust that nothing touches my life without passing through Your love and purpose.

Thank You that You redeem my life from trouble. In famine, You will preserve me. In war, You will shield me. I don't have to live in fear of destruction, because You are my Defender and Provider.

Keep me from the fear of harm, even when the world shakes. Let Your peace guard my heart. Cover me with Your protection, and remind me that I am never alone—You are near, You are faithful, and You are enough.

In Jesus' name,
Amen.

Day 11: Call and I Will Answer

Call on me in the day of trouble. I will deliver you, and you will honor me."
—Psalms 50:15 WEB

Gracious God,

I call on You in the day of trouble, and You answer me. Thank You for hearing my cries and for being near when I need You most. When I am overwhelmed, You are my refuge and strength.

Help me to trust You more each day, to seek You not just in times of trouble but always. Teach me to live in a way that honors You, knowing You are my Deliverer and my Savior.

I put my hope in Your unfailing love and mercy. Rescue me, Lord, and sustain me by Your mighty hand.

In Jesus' name,
Amen.

Day 12: TOO WEAK TO FIGHT, STRONG ENOUGH TO PRAY

> They said to him, "Thus says Hezekiah, 'Today is a day of trouble, of rebuke, and of rejection; for the children have come to the point of birth, and there is no strength to deliver them. It may be Yahweh your God will hear all the words of Rabshakeh, whom the king of Assyria his master has sent to defy the living God, and will rebuke the words which Yahweh your God has heard. Therefore lift up your prayer for the remnant that is left.'"
> —2 Kings 19:3-4 WEB

Sovereign Lord,

There are moments when I feel like this is a day of trouble, of rebuke, and of deep uncertainty—just like in the days of King Hezekiah. I feel weak, like there's no strength left to push forward. But just as Hezekiah turned to You, so do I.

Lord, You have heard the threats, the fears, the words meant to shake my faith. But You are greater. You are the God who sees and who defends. I ask You to rebuke what stands against Your purpose in my life. Silence the voice of the enemy and rise up in power.

Have mercy, O God. Strengthen me in the midst of this battle. Speak a word that brings life, peace, and deliverance. Let me see Your hand move, not just for my sake—but for the honor of Your great name.

In Jesus' name,
Amen.

Day 13: When the Night Won't End

For the Chief Musician. To Jeduthun. A Psalm by Asaph. My cry goes to God! Indeed, I cry to God for help, and for him to listen to me. In the day of my trouble I sought the Lord. My hand was stretched out in the night, and didn't get tired. My soul refused to be comforted.
—Psalms 77:1-2 WEB

O Lord my God,

With my voice I cry out to You—because I know You hear me. In the day of my trouble, I seek You. My hands are stretched out in the night, longing for Your touch, for Your peace. My soul refuses to be comforted by anything but You.

Sometimes, the pain lingers. Sometimes, the answers feel delayed. But still, I come. Still, I call. Because You are my only hope, my only help, my only healing.

Draw near to me, Lord. Speak to the silence. Strengthen my heart when it feels faint. I will wait on You, trusting that even in the darkness, You are at work.

In Jesus' name,
Amen.

Day 14: May God Meet You There

For the Chief Musician. A Psalm by David. May Yahweh answer you in the day of trouble. May the name of the God of Jacob set you up on high, send you help from the sanctuary, grant you support from Zion, remember all your offerings, and accept your burned sacrifice. Selah. May He grant you your heart's desire, and fulfill all your counsel.
—Psalms 20:1-4 WEB

Faithful God,

May You hear me in the day of trouble. When my heart is heavy and the path uncertain, I look to You. Let the name of the God of Jacob defend me—stand between me and every enemy, seen and unseen.

Send me help from Your sanctuary, and strengthen me out of Zion. I need more than human answers—I need Your presence, Your wisdom, Your power. Remember my prayers, my sacrifices, my surrender, and receive them with grace.

Grant me the desires of my heart, Lord—not just what I want, but what You will. Fulfill every purpose You have placed within me. Let my life reflect Your goodness and bring You glory.

In Jesus' name,
Amen.

Day 15: SAFE IN HIS NAME

> Yahweh will also be a high tower for the oppressed; a high tower in times of trouble. Those who know your name will put their trust in you, for you, Yahweh, have not forsaken those who seek you.
> —Psalms 9:9-10 WEB

Mighty Refuge,

You are a stronghold for the oppressed, a safe place in times of trouble. When everything feels unstable, You remain unshaken. You are close to the broken-hearted, and I thank You that I can run to You and be safe.

Lord, I put my trust in You. I know Your name, and I believe in Your faithfulness. You have never forsaken those who seek You—and You won't start now. Help me to rest in that truth when fear tries to take hold.

Be my shelter, my strength, and my peace. Let me cling to You in every season, knowing You are always near.

In Jesus' name,
Amen.

Day 16: UNSHAKEN IN THE STORM

For the Chief Musician. By the sons of Korah. According to Alamoth. God is our refuge and strength, a very present help in trouble. Therefore we won't be afraid, though the earth changes, though the mountains are shaken into the heart of the seas; though its waters roar and are troubled, though the mountains tremble with their swelling. Selah. There is a river, the streams of which make the city of God glad, the holy place of the tents of the Most High. God is within her. She shall not be moved. God will help her at dawn.
—Psalms 46:1-5 WEB

God, my Refuge and Strength,

You are always present—especially in trouble. You are my help, my steady ground when the world feels like it's falling apart. Even if the earth shakes, even if the mountains crumble into the sea, I will not fear. Because You are with me.

Let the waters roar, let the nations rage—Your presence is greater. There is a river of peace that flows from Your heart, and it makes my soul glad. You dwell in the midst of Your people, and because You are here, I will not be moved.

At the break of day, You will help me. You are faithful, unshaken, and forever near.

In Jesus' name,
Amen.

Day 17: LIFTED HIGH, HELD CLOSE

> For in the day of trouble, he will keep me secretly in his pavilion. In the secret place of his tabernacle, he will hide me. He will lift me up on a rock. Now my head will be lifted up above my enemies around me; I will offer sacrifices of joy in his tent. I will sing, yes, I will sing praises to Yahweh.
> —Psalms 27:5-6 WEB

Lord,

In the day of trouble, You hide me in Your shelter. You lift me above the chaos, above the fear, and place me safely in the secret place of Your presence. When everything around me feels uncertain, You are my steady refuge.

You set me high upon a rock, and I know I am secure in You. My head is lifted above my enemies—not because of my strength, but because of Yours. So I will offer praise with joy, even in the waiting. I will sing to You, because You are faithful.

Thank You for being my hiding place, my fortress, and my song.

In Jesus' name,
Amen.

Day 18: STRENGTH IN THE STRUGGLE

> But the salvation of the righteous is from Yahweh. He is their stronghold in the time of trouble. Yahweh helps them, and rescues them. He rescues them from the wicked, and saves them, Because they have taken refuge in him.
> —Psalms 37:39-40 WEB

Faithful Deliverer,

My salvation comes from You alone. You are my strength in times of trouble—my protector when the weight of life feels too heavy to carry. You see every struggle, every silent cry, and You do not turn away.

You help me and deliver me—not because I am perfect, but because I trust in You. You rescue me from harm and guard me from the traps I can't even see. You are my safe place, my shield, and my hope.

Teach me to rest in Your promises. Strengthen my heart to keep trusting, even when the road is hard. You are always with me, and You will not fail.

In Jesus' name,
Amen.

Day 19: Blessed to Bless

> *For the Chief Musician. A Psalm by David.* Blessed is he who considers the poor. Yahweh will deliver him in the day of evil. Yahweh will preserve him, and keep him alive. He shall be blessed on the earth, and he will not surrender him to the will of his enemies.
> —Psalms 41:1-2 WEB

Compassionate Lord,

You see those who care for the poor and the weak, and You promise blessing over their lives. Help me to live with a heart of compassion—open to the needs of others, just as You have been merciful to me.

Thank You that when trouble comes, You will deliver me. You will protect me, keep me alive, and bless me in the land of the living. You will not hand me over to the plans of the enemy, because You are my Defender.

Let my life be marked by kindness and justice, and may I reflect Your love in all I do.

In Jesus' name,
Amen.

Day 20: Freedom is Coming

> For Yahweh says: "We have heard a voice of trembling; a voice of fear, and not of peace. Ask now, and see whether a man travails with child. Why do I see every man with his hands on his waist, as a woman in travail, and all faces are turned pale? Alas! for that day is great, so that none is like it. It is even the time of Jacob's trouble; but he will be saved out of it. It will come to pass in that day, says Yahweh of Armies, that I will break his yoke from off your neck, and will burst your bonds. Strangers will no more make them their bondservants; but they will serve Yahweh their God, and David their king, whom I will raise up to them. Therefore don't be afraid, O Jacob my servant, says Yahweh. Don't be dismayed, Israel. For, behold, I will save you from afar, and save your offspring from the land of their captivity. Jacob will return, and will be quiet and at ease. No one will make him afraid.
> —Jeremiah 30:5-10 WEB

Almighty God,

You have spoken of a time of great distress—a day of trembling and fear, like none before. But even in the darkness, You offer a promise of hope. Though the cries of anguish rise, You are not absent. You see, You know, and You are still in control.

You told Your people not to be afraid, not to be dismayed, because You are with them. And so today, I hold on to that same truth. Though trouble may surround me, though fear may try to rise, I will not be shaken—for You are near.

Thank You for the promise of restoration. You are the God who breaks chains, who saves from distant places, who brings peace where there was fear. I trust in Your power to deliver, to heal, and to bring me into freedom.

In Jesus' name,
Amen.

Day 21: Hope in the Silence

> *For the Chief Musician. A Psalm by David.* How long, Yahweh? Will you forget me forever? How long will you hide your face from me? How long shall I take counsel in my soul, having sorrow in my heart every day? How long shall my enemy triumph over me? Behold, and answer me, Yahweh, my God. Give light to my eyes, lest I sleep in death; Lest my enemy say, "I have prevailed against him;" Lest my adversaries rejoice when I fall. But I trust in your loving kindness. My heart rejoices in your salvation. I will sing to Yahweh, because he has been good to me.
> —Psalms 13:1-6 WEB

O Lord,

How long will You forget me? It feels like silence stretches on, and I'm left with questions and sorrow in my heart every day. How long will I wrestle with these thoughts? How long will it feel like the darkness is winning?

But still—I lift my eyes to You. I ask You to consider me, to answer me. Light up my eyes, Lord, lest I fall into despair. Don't let the enemy rejoice over my weakness. Don't let the shadows have the last word.

I choose to trust in Your mercy. Even when I can't see the way, I will hold on to the hope of Your unfailing love. I will rejoice in Your salvation—because You have been good to me, even in the waiting.

In Jesus' name,
Amen.

Day 22: Lift Me from the Gates

> Have mercy on me, Yahweh. See my affliction by those who hate me, and lift me up from the gates of death; that I may show all of your praise. In the gates of the daughter of Zion, I will rejoice in your salvation.
> —Psalms 9:13-14 WEB

Lord, You see me—right here in the middle of my need. You know the pain I carry and the sorrow that lingers in the corners of my heart. Have mercy on me, O Lord. I'm asking You, just like David did, to look on my suffering and lift me out of this place of despair.

You are the One who rescues me from the gates of death. Only You can breathe life back into these weary bones and renew the hope I thought I'd lost. You have saved me before, and I believe You can do it again. I trust You—not just with my circumstances, but with my heart.

If You lift me up, I will lift You up. I will praise You with all I have. I'll speak of Your goodness even in the valley. I'll rejoice in who You are—not just because things are easy, but because You are faithful, strong, and near. You are the God who sees, who saves, and who never lets go.

I surrender my fear, my hurt, and my doubt into Your hands. Replace them with songs of joy. Let my life be a testimony at the gates of Your Daughter Zion, where the broken find healing, and the lost find home.

Thank You for being my Rescuer and my reason to rejoice.

In Jesus' name, Amen.

Day 23: Mercy in My Mess

> Now therefore, our God, the great, the mighty, and the awesome God, who keeps covenant and loving kindness, don't let all the travail seem little before you, that has come on us, on our kings, on our princes, on our priests, on our prophets, on our fathers, and on all your people, since the time of the kings of Assyria to this day. However you are just in all that has come on us; for you have dealt truly, but we have done wickedly.
> —Nehemiah 9:32-33 WEB

God of mercy and might,

You are the great Deliverer—the faithful One who keeps covenant and shows unfailing love, even when we don't. You have never abandoned Your people, and You will not abandon me now. You are righteous in all that You do. Even when trouble comes, I know You are still just, still good, still in control.

Lord, I confess that much of my trouble has been tangled with my own choices, my own pride, and forgetfulness of You. But even in discipline, You are compassionate. Even in hardship, You are near. You are not cruel or distant—You are holy, and You act with perfect justice.

I cry out to You now—not as someone who deserves deliverance, but as someone desperate for it. I ask not because I'm worthy, but because You are merciful. You've delivered Your people before. You've shown grace to generations. So I trust that You can lift me too.

Rescue me, Lord—not just from my situation, but from every chain that holds me back from walking fully with You. Teach me to walk in

Your truth, even when the road is hard. Let my deliverance bring You glory.

In Jesus' name, Amen.

Day 24: Refuge in the Tears

> I will be glad and rejoice in your loving kindness, for you have seen my affliction. You have known my soul in adversities. You have not shut me up into the hand of the enemy. You have set my feet in a large place. Have mercy on me, Yahweh, for I am in distress. My eye, my soul, and my body waste away with grief.
> —Psalms 31:7-9 WEB

Heavenly Father,

I will rejoice and be glad in Your unfailing love, because You see me. You don't overlook my pain or ignore my tears. You know the depths of my trouble—the ache in my chest, the weariness in my soul. Nothing is hidden from You. And still, You choose to love me. Still, You hold me close.

You've seen my suffering, Lord. You've watched as sorrow wrapped around my heart, and You've never turned away. I praise You because even in my weakness, You are my strength. Even when I feel surrounded, You are my refuge.

Right now, God, I'm asking You again—have mercy on me. Trouble presses in, and I feel worn thin. My eyes are tired from crying, my soul feels crushed beneath the weight. But I turn to You, because You are the God who delivers, who restores, who saves.

Lift me up out of this heaviness. Hold me steady in the middle of the storm. Let me feel Your presence like sunlight breaking through the clouds. I trust You—not because life is easy, but because You are always faithful.

You are my Deliverer. And I will praise You in the valley just as I would on the mountain.

In Jesus' name, Amen.

Day 25: Trust Through the Trial

> Our fathers trusted in you. They trusted, and you delivered them. They cried to you, and were delivered. They trusted in you, and were not disappointed. But I am a worm, and no man; a reproach of men, and despised by the people. All those who see me mock me. They insult me with their lips. They shake their heads, saying, "He trusts in Yahweh. Let him deliver him. Let him rescue him, since he delights in him." But you brought me out of the womb. You made me trust while at my mother's breasts. I was thrown on you from my mother's womb. You are my God since my mother bore me. Don't be far from me, for trouble is near. For there is no one to help.
> —Psalms 22:4-11 WEB

Lord,

You have always been the God who saves. Our ancestors trusted You—and You came through. They cried out, and You delivered. They leaned on You, and they were never put to shame. And now, here I am, crying out too.

I feel so small, so worn down by trouble. People may not see the depth of my struggle, but You do. You've been my God since the beginning. From the moment I was born, You've been near. You brought me into this world, and You've never let me go.

So don't leave me now, Lord. Trouble is closing in, and I feel like I have nothing left. But I know You are faithful. I've heard it, I've read it, and deep down, I believe it.

I'm choosing to trust You—not because I feel strong, but because You are. Not because I understand everything, but because You've always been with me. Stay close, God. Be my refuge. Deliver me like You've delivered so many before me.

In Jesus' name, Amen.

Day 26: Rise Up, God

> Why do you stand far off, Yahweh? Why do you hide yourself in times of trouble? Arise, Yahweh! God, lift up your hand! Don't forget the helpless.
> —Psalms 10:1,12 WEB

Lord,

Sometimes it feels like You're far away—like You're hiding while I struggle. I look around at all the trouble, and I wonder why You're silent. My heart aches with questions, but still, I lift my eyes to You.

Rise up, Lord. Don't let injustice win. Don't let the broken go unseen. I know You are not blind to pain or deaf to prayer. So I'm asking You—move in power. Show up in the middle of the mess.

You are the God who sees. The God who hears. The God who delivers. So I won't stop praying, even when it's hard. I won't stop believing that You care, even when I can't feel it.

I put my hope in You—not in what I see, but in who You are. Rise up, Lord, and let Your justice and mercy flood this trouble with light.

In Jesus' name, Amen.

Day 27: Not a Stranger to My Sorrow

> You hope of Israel, its Savior in the time of trouble, why should you be as a foreigner in the land, and as a wayfaring man who turns aside to stay for a night? Why should you be like a scared man, as a mighty man who can't save? Yet you, Yahweh, are in the middle of us, and we are called by your name. Don't leave us.
> —Jeremiah 14:8-9 WEB

O Lord,

You are the hope of Israel—the One who saves in times of trouble. And right now, I need You. Don't be a stranger to me. Don't feel like a traveler just passing through or a warrior too tired to fight. You are not distant. You are not weak. You are near, and You are mighty.

Even when it feels like You're silent, I believe You are still with me. You've called me Your own, and I belong to You. So I'm clinging to that truth, even in the silence, even in the storm.

Show Yourself strong, God. Be who You've always been—my Defender, my Rescuer, my Deliverer. Don't let this trouble shake my faith. Remind me that You are still on the throne, still in control, still my God.

I trust You. Even when I don't understand, I choose to trust You.

In Jesus' name, Amen.

Day 28: BEAUTY FOR ASHES

> Instead of your shame you will have double. Instead of dishonor, they will rejoice in their portion. Therefore in their land, they will possess double. Everlasting joy will be to them.
> —Isaiah 61:7 WEB

Lord,

You see every loss, every tear, every shame I've carried. And yet, You promise beauty for ashes, and joy where there was sorrow. You don't just patch up the broken places—you restore them with abundance. Where I've felt dishonored, You offer a double portion. Where I've been wounded, You promise everlasting joy.

I bring You my pain, Lord—the regrets, the rejection, the moments that made me feel less than. And I receive Your promise: that You will give me back more than what was stolen. Not because I deserve it, but because You are good.

Let this be the beginning of healing in me. Let Your joy take root where despair once lived. I trust that You are a God of redemption, and You're not done writing my story.

Thank You for turning my shame into praise.

In Jesus' name, Amen.

Day 29: DOUBLE FOR MY TROUBLE

> Turn to the stronghold, you prisoners of hope! Even today I declare that I will restore double to you.
> —Zechariah 9:12 WEB

Faithful God,

Today I return to You—my stronghold, my refuge, my safe place. I come not with strength, but as a prisoner of hope. Even in the waiting, I choose to hope. Even in the pain, I believe You will restore.

You see every battle I've fought, every tear I've cried, and You promise to repay with blessing—double for my trouble. Not just relief, but redemption. Not just survival, but restoration.

So I hold on. I hold on to Your Word, to Your heart, to the hope that You are still working behind the scenes. You are the God who remembers, the God who rebuilds, the God who restores.

Thank You for being my stronghold in the storm. I may feel weak, but in You, I am never alone.

In Jesus' name, Amen.

Day 30: Restored by Grace

> Yahweh turned the captivity of Job, when he prayed for his friends. Yahweh gave Job twice as much as he had before.
> —Job 42:10 WEB

Father,

You are the God who restores. Like Job, I've walked through seasons of deep loss and confusion. I've cried, questioned, and waited in the silence. Yet Your Word says that when Job prayed for others, You turned his situation around and gave him more than before.

Lord, I choose to believe You can do the same for me. I surrender my pain, my disappointments, and the things I don't understand. I lay down resentment and choose to forgive. Help me pray with a heart that trusts You—even when it still hurts.

You are my Deliverer, and I believe that restoration is possible because of who You are. Bring healing where there's been brokenness, joy where sorrow has lived too long, and hope where I've felt empty.

Thank You that You are not finished with my story. What You allow, You also redeem. I trust You to work all things together for good.

In Jesus' name, Amen.

Day 31: Refined and Redeemed

> For you, God, have tested us. You have refined us, as silver is refined. You brought us into prison. You laid a burden on our backs. You allowed men to ride over our heads. We went through fire and through water, but you brought us to the place of abundance. I will come into your temple with burnt offerings. I will pay my vows to you, which my lips promised, and my mouth spoke, when I was in distress.
> —Psalms 66:10-14 WEB

Lord,

You have tested me like silver refined in fire. You allowed me to walk through trials I didn't choose—through pressure, pain, and places that felt like prisons. I've known what it is to feel burdened and stretched beyond my strength. But through it all, You were purifying me. You didn't abandon me.

You brought me through fire and water—and now, You are leading me into a place of abundance. I see now that even my struggle had purpose. You were shaping my heart to trust You more deeply.

So I come to You, not just with words, but with a life laid down. Like the psalmist, I offer what I vowed in the darkness—my praise, my surrender, my devotion. I remember what I promised when I was in trouble, and I bring it to You now with thanksgiving.

You are faithful. You have delivered me. You are still delivering me. And I will keep my promises, because You kept Yours.

In Jesus' name, Amen.

Day 32: Hope Beyond the Dust

"Man, who is born of a woman, is of few days, and full of trouble. He grows up like a flower, and is cut down. He also flees like a shadow, and doesn't continue. Do you open your eyes on such a one, and bring me into judgment with you? Who can bring a clean thing out of an unclean? Not one. Seeing his days are determined, the number of his months is with you, and you have appointed his bounds that he can't pass; Look away from him, that he may rest, until he shall accomplish, as a hireling, his day. "For there is hope for a tree, If it is cut down, that it will sprout again, that the tender branch of it will not cease. Though its root grows old in the earth, and its stock dies in the ground, yet through the scent of water it will bud, and sprout boughs like a plant.
—Job 14:1-9 WEB

Lord,

You know how fragile my life is—how short my days are and how full of trouble they can be. I feel the weight of my weakness, like a flower that withers or a shadow that fades. Sometimes it feels like You're watching too closely, examining every fault, and I wonder how I can stand before You.

But even as I wrestle with these thoughts, I look to the hope You've planted in creation itself. Just as a tree cut down can sprout again, and new life can grow from what seemed dead, so I believe You can bring renewal to me.

Though I feel worn down, You are the God of hope. At the scent of water, the tree comes back to life—and at the touch of Your Spirit, so can I. I don't have all the answers. I don't see the full picture. But I trust in Your mercy, in Your power to revive what has been broken.

Let new life rise in me, Lord. Bring beauty from my pain, and give me strength to hope again, even in the dust.

In Jesus' name, Amen.

Day 33: Peace in the Quiet

> When he gives quietness, who then can condemn [make trouble (KJV)]? When he hides his face, who then can see him? Alike whether to a nation, or to a man,
> —Job 34:29 WEB

Father,

When You bring quietness, who can make trouble? When You choose to hide Your face, no one can find You. Yet even in silence, You are sovereign. Even when I cannot see what You are doing, I know You are still in control.

So I rest in Your covering. When the world feels unstable and voices around me are loud, I lean into the peace that only You can give. You silence chaos with a word. You guard the righteous and judge with perfect wisdom.

Thank You for being my refuge when I feel uncertain. You hold power over nations and individuals alike. Nothing escapes Your notice. Nothing can move without Your permission.

So I trust You—when You speak and when You are still. I trust that Your quietness is not absence, but protection. Your hiddenness is not neglect, but mercy. You are working all things according to Your will.

Keep me under Your hand, Lord. Let Your peace surround me and Your justice sustain me, until the day You bring all things into the light.

In Jesus' name, Amen.

Day 34: Songs from the Wilderness

> "Therefore behold, I will allure her, and bring her into the wilderness, and speak tenderly to her. I will give her vineyards from there, and the valley of Achor for a door of hope; and she will respond there, as in the days of her youth, and as in the day when she came up out of the land of Egypt.
> —Hosea 2:14-15 WEB

Lord,

Thank You for Your mercy that pursues me, even when I've wandered far. You don't cast me off—you lead me into the wilderness to speak tenderly to my heart. In the barren places, where everything else is stripped away, You draw me closer to Yourself.

Thank You for not giving up on me. You transform the valley of trouble into a door of hope. Where there was sorrow, You plant songs of joy. Where I felt lost, You call me beloved again.

Teach me to listen for Your voice in the quiet. Help me to trust that even in the wilderness, You are at work—healing, restoring, preparing me for something new. You are the God who brings life from desolation, and You've promised to turn my trouble into triumph.

I will answer You there, like in the days of my first love, with a heart renewed and surrendered. Thank You for Your relentless love and gentle leading.

In Jesus' name, Amen.

Day 35: VALLEY OF REST

> Sharon will be a fold of flocks, and the valley of Achor a place for herds to lie down in[1], for my people who have sought me.
> —Isaiah 65:10 WEB

Lord,

You are my Shepherd, and in You I find rest. When everything feels dry and desolate, You promise to make a place of peace—You turn valleys into pastures and weary hearts into gardens of delight.

You have said that Sharon will become a fold for flocks and the Valley of Achor a resting place for those who seek You. I come to seek You now. Even in the midst of trouble, I believe You are preparing a place of quiet for me.

Thank You for making room for the faithful. Thank You for turning hardship into habitation—for turning my trials into testimony. I long to dwell where Your presence is, where my soul can breathe again and hope can rise.

Lead me, Lord, into that promised rest. Settle my heart in Your love. Let me lie down in Your care and rise again with renewed strength.

In Jesus' name, Amen.

---

[1] Easton's Bible Dictionary: *"The valley of Achor, a place for herds to lie down in;"* i.e., that which had been a source of calamity would become a source of blessing.

Day 36: Faithful Way Out

> No temptation has taken you except what is common to man. God is faithful, who will not allow you to be tempted above what you are able, but will with the temptation also make the way of escape, that you may be able to endure it.
> —1 Corinthians 10:13 WEB

Faithful God,

You know my struggles. You see the temptations I face, the pressure that weighs on me, the moments when I feel like giving in. But Your Word reminds me that I'm not alone—what I'm facing isn't beyond what others have faced, and more importantly, it's not beyond what You can handle.

You are faithful. You promised that You won't let me be tested beyond what I can bear. Even when the trial feels overwhelming, You've already made a way out—a path to stand firm.

Help me look for that way, Lord. Help me trust that it's there, even when I can't see it right away. Strengthen my heart when I feel weak. Remind me that by Your Spirit, I am not powerless. You are my strength, my shield, my deliverer.

Thank You for being the God who never abandons, who never tempts, and who always provides. In every test, You are with me. In every trial, You are enough.

I choose to trust You. I choose to stand.

In Jesus' name, Amen.

Day 37: POWER IN THE PRESSURE

> We are pressed on every side, yet not crushed; perplexed, yet not to despair; pursued, yet not forsaken; struck down, yet not destroyed; always carrying in the body the putting to death of the Lord Jesus, that the life of Jesus may also be revealed in our body. For we who live are always delivered to death for Jesus' sake, that the life also of Jesus may be revealed in our mortal flesh.
> —2 Corinthians 4:8-11 WEB

Lord, sometimes I feel pressed on every side—by sorrow, stress, or fear—but Your Word says I am not crushed. I may be perplexed, but I am not in despair. Struck down, but not destroyed. These trials are real, but so is Your power in me.

Thank You for sustaining me when I feel weak. Even when I carry death in my body—the weight of suffering or struggle—I know the life of Jesus is also at work within me. Every hardship I face becomes a place where Your resurrection power can shine.

Help me not to lose heart. Let my life reflect Your glory, even in pain. Let others see that it is You who keeps me standing. I surrender this fragile body, this cracked vessel, into Your hands. Use it for Your purpose.

May the life of Jesus be revealed in me—through the hard days and through the healing ones. I trust that what's dying in me is making room for what You are raising up.

In Jesus' name, Amen.

Day 38: Comfort for the Weary

> For even when we had come into Macedonia, our flesh had no relief, but we were afflicted on every side. Fightings were outside. Fear was inside. Nevertheless, he who comforts the lowly, God, comforted us by the coming of Titus; and not by his coming only, but also by the comfort with which he was comforted in you, while he told us of your longing, your mourning, and your zeal for me; so that I rejoiced still more.
> —2 Corinthians 7:5-7 WEB

Lord, You know the battles I face—within and without. Like Paul, I've had moments when my heart was weary, my mind anxious, and my spirit low. Conflict around me, fear inside me—sometimes it feels like too much.

But You are the God who comforts the downcast. You see me in my heaviness, and You send help. Whether through a word of encouragement, the presence of a friend, or the quiet nearness of Your Spirit, You lift me up when I can't lift myself.

Thank You for knowing exactly how to reach me. Thank You for the people You've sent at just the right time—those who have refreshed my spirit and reminded me I'm not alone.

Even in my low places, You are faithful. You bring comfort, not just to remove my pain, but to renew my courage. So I open my heart to You again. Fill me with peace. Strengthen me with hope.

You are my refuge, my comfort, my joy—especially in the dark places.

In Jesus' name, Amen.

Day 39: CRUSHED BUT CARRIED

> For we don't desire to have you uninformed, brothers, concerning our affliction which happened to us in Asia, that we were weighed down exceedingly, beyond our power, so much that we despaired even of life. Yes, we ourselves have had the sentence of death within ourselves, that we should not trust in ourselves, but in God who raises the dead, who delivered us out of so great a death, and does deliver; on whom we have set our hope that he will also still deliver us; you also helping together on our behalf by your supplication; that, for the gift given to us by means of many, thanks may be given by many persons on your behalf.
> —2 Corinthians 1:8-11 WEB

Father, I come to You today with a heart that remembers what it feels like to be burdened beyond my own strength. There have been moments where I've felt crushed—pressed down under the weight of trials, with no escape in sight. Like Paul, I have despaired even of life itself. But in those moments, You have drawn me closer, teaching me not to rely on myself, but on You—the God who raises the dead.

You are the Deliverer. You have delivered me before, and I believe You will deliver me again. I lift my eyes to You, knowing that my hope is not empty. You are the God of all comfort, and You comfort me even in the middle of affliction, so I can encourage others when they suffer. Your mercy flows freely, and Your power is made perfect in weakness.

I thank You for the prayers of others—how You use the intercession of fellow believers to surround me with grace. Their prayers are part of my deliverance, and together we give thanks for Your faithfulness. You don't waste suffering; You transform it into a testimony of Your power.

So I surrender again to Your plan. I place my trust not in my own understanding, but in Your goodness. You are the One who holds my life, and You are not done with my story. I will continue to hope in You, for You are able to do immeasurably more than I can imagine—even in the darkest seasons.

In Jesus' name, Amen.

Day 40: When Trouble Finds Me

> For affliction doesn't come out of the dust, neither does trouble spring out of the ground; but man is born to trouble, as the sparks fly upward. "But as for me, I would seek God. I would commit my cause to God, who does great things that can't be fathomed, marvelous things without number;
> —Job 5:6-9 WEB

Lord, I rest in the truth that trouble does not sprout from the soil, and hardship does not grow like weeds from the ground. My pain is not random—You are sovereign over all things. Even when sorrow finds me, I know You have not abandoned me. You are not the author of chaos; You are the God who performs wonders that cannot be counted.

You see what I cannot. You reach into the depths of suffering and draw out purpose, healing, and hope. Your works are great and unsearchable, and though I don't always understand, I choose to trust. You are doing more than I can see. You stretch the skies and shake the earth. You lift the humble and bring rain upon dry ground. Nothing is too hard for You.

So I lay down my fear, my confusion, and my questions, and I choose to believe that You are still working in my trouble. You are the God who redeems, who restores, who delivers. Your ways are higher, and I put my hope in You.

In Jesus' name, Amen.

Epilogue

You've made it through 40 days of seeking, praying, and pressing into the presence of God through the storms of life. That in itself is a testimony—a quiet yet powerful act of faith that says, *"God, I'm still here. I'm still reaching for You."*

Maybe you've felt His nearness in fresh ways. Maybe you're still waiting for the breakthrough. Either way, know this: your prayers have not been wasted, and your cries have not been ignored. The God who hears your voice in the valley is the same God who walks with you to the other side.

Deliverance isn't always instant, but it is always certain when you're walking with the Deliverer. Sometimes He changes your situation. Other times, He changes *you* in the middle of it. But He never leaves. And He always redeems.

As you go forward, carry these truths with you:

- You are not forgotten.
- Trouble does not define your future.
- God's promises are greater than your pain.
- Prayer is your constant connection to the One who holds all things together.

Let these 40 days mark a beginning, not an end. Keep opening your heart. Keep returning to Scripture. Keep praying—even if it's messy or simple or quiet. God treasures your voice.

And when life feels overwhelming again (because it will), return to these pages or open a fresh one with Him. He is still writing your story—and He writes in grace, not fear.

May you continue to walk in peace, strengthened by His Word, surrounded by His mercy, and delivered by His love.

With hope and prayer,
Cyril Opoku

Encourage Others with Your Story

If this book has encouraged or strengthened you in your journey toward deliverance, I would be grateful if you could share your experience by leaving a review on Amazon. Your honest feedback not only helps me grow but also encourages others seeking God's protection and peace to find hope through these prayers and Scriptures.

Thank you for letting this book be part of your walk with God. May His deliverance continue to surround you every day!

More from PrayerScripts

SCRIPTURES & PRAYERS FOR DELIVERANCE FROM EVIL: 50 DAYS OF PRAYER TO OVERCOME DARKNESS AND FIND GOD'S PROTECTION

When darkness presses in, how do you pray?

When fear grips your heart or unseen battles rage around you, you need more than generic words—you need Scripture, truth, and the steady hand of God to lead you through.

Scriptures & Prayers for Deliverance from Evil: 50 Days of Prayer to Overcome Darkness and Find God's Protection is a powerful devotional journey designed to help you pray boldly and biblically through seasons of spiritual warfare, oppression, fear, or uncertainty.